Bird Song

and

Nectar in the Silences

how we are and how we will be

by

Lisa Lopresti

First published 2022 by The Hedgehog Poetry Press

Published in the UK by
The Hedgehog Poetry Press
5, Coppack House
Churchill Avenue
Clevedon
BS21 6QW

www.hedgehogpress.co.uk

ISBN: 978-1-913499-49-5

A CIP Catalogue record for this book is available from the British Library.

Cover Image is by Mrs Doris E Luxton my Grandmother, Mary Caldwell's friend.

In memory of my 2 Grandmothers, who were both Mary's,

as is my middle name.

Mary Harkin and Mary Caldwell.

They were so different but dignified and remembered.

'The poems are sensual;

they sing with positivity'

- Pauline Sewards

Contents

WE ARE WHO WE ARE...

intricate and as light as a bee's wing
she bumbles through life in dappled sunlight

harvest mouse smiles for the change of seasons
dampened by the life that corrals us into categories

but she hovers above this abyss
without ever looking at who is looking back

hydrangea blue depends on where you are rooted
as all that is natural   exists.

ROSE BOMBS

Inspired by the Arabic musician Maya Youssef 'bombs turn into roses' she said' I heal and I surrender. May the white petals of peace fall on Syria.'

Maya Youssef spoke to me about war,
I felt the gravity of tragedy
as never before
in this moment of notes.

She hopes that bombs turn into roses
qanun whispered maqam to my western ears.
Floating flakes of red and white rose buds,
poignantly soft,

with sequestered air to breathe between.
High and low thrumming cords of danger,
sirocco dust blushing the blooms,
in fickle directions.

Then building in fear and fragrance
petal light fingers on strings
of anger and loss again,
before soothing rose water

sweetens wars metallic scythe edge,
with birdsong and nectar in the silences.

THE ANSWERS

prayers are the language of belief
the poetic reiteration of the
known that is held in your heart

the steppingstones of hope
                    without doubt
                              reaching out
                      in acceptance and joy
                                    to the other

you and me
in the same city
both daughters of immigrants

the heartbeat of poetry
in our faiths
asking questions of our answers

BESEECHING

Prevalence of longing glances,
under lashes
soul searching flashes.
Beseeching lighthouse pulses,
urgency of the messages
Always, missed by the beholder.

The agony of loving,
without being loved.
Impossibility of joy,
is the pain of the lonely heart.

Bittersweet –
as apart there is no beginning:
and so there is no end.

I FADE FROM PICTURES

now. Before, my direct gaze
was Atlantic blue arched by corn rows
hazel tensile youth

I swayed with the breeze
and the willow wisps of my hair
which were playfully entwined

by the light touch of his fingers
his heat too close to the sand dunes
of my curves, the pebble ridge of

my back, the dolphin of my
heart, in its iron rich sea,
us moving away, my gaze adverted

in a silver flash of a shoal
I darted, quickly
my blushing flamingo neck

remembering my own responsibility
though polaroid colours wane
you can see, we   wore   laden   cloaks.

TAKE THE STARS...

Take the stars, in jars,
the sun in our butter,
moon beams through net curtains,
and sea sounds in seashells.
Hold these close in memory,
the items in our house.
To touch, remember and
smooth the boredom
wrinkles
as worry and inaction
separates us from the ones most loved.
Ironically social media bringing
us virtually together,
if you ignore the bitter
vitriol of fiends
wielding blue thumbs ups
with acid words
who must walk among us
with the invisibility of a sociopath's smile
now often cloaked in masks.
You can hear, the hack of magpies.

PORTISHEAD

Sat on the poured concrete bench, I wait for you. In front of the Lido the sun sinks to adorn its reflective sunglasses, burnishing the estuary to brass. Strolling families maunder and meander around the lake and the small ones shoot and pitch below elbows and around ankles. In indigo, firecracker car door slams and engine whir fade the people gone. A single grey smoke cloud in the cyan evenfall polishes the scimitar edge of the waning crescent moon, as a man at arms to guard against the blind of the darkening night sky. Is it hiding more than night and day?

YOU NEVER CRY ALONE

The sky can feel like me,
populated with pretty particles
of clouds to make an elevated sea
in the mind of the atmosphere.
White and periwinkle,
soft to the hard blue clear to see.
This is why the clouds in days gone by,
were attributed to
cotton cradles,
myth fables,
cushions to the gods,
or racing friend of the moon,
magical floating sad silver,
tarnished balloon.
Cumulus moving slow or fast,
without mass
but crackling with electricity,
guttural roars of the atmosphere,
Storms personality.
Moody blues and purple bruise,
brooding frowns bearing down.
Granite, plum, steel, white, peach, pink,
cheerful skies for the sun to chink
through gloom with yellow,
the happy fellow,
and every shade in-between
strata, layers.
Flat, rounded, wisps,
mountain clippers,
candy floss dippers.
Unending individuality,
changing sky tapestry.

It's lonely without a cloud.
A cloud means you never have to cry alone.

LOVE IS THE SPIRIT OF A CAT

There is no choice in love.
You can decide to declare or not declare
your feelings, to devote or decline time
with whom you love.

To claw against your feelings,
or act or not to act upon them. To be
swept away or turn away, hissing regret,
but you have no choice in love,

your feelings are the spirit
of a cat, who imperiously does their own
thing, in their own time, without logic
or instruction.

VIRULENCE OF CORVIDS

their cries slick over the sky
as in 'Battle of Britain' formations
they fly
with murderous intent to roost
in their favourite copse of tree's

dawn and dusk have riotous wing beats
and 'West Side Story' conflicts
they clip
short, self-aware about the
needs of the colonies gauntlet

of survival, their obsidian council
a 'Life of Pi' imagination
they blazon
into loud joyous, raucous abandon
when they meet to screech and sleep

CAPITAL VISITS AFTER LOCKDOWN

Buildings
with stories to tell, monolithic grandeur,
Rome of our day. Shoaling crowds move between
great monuments
on a grand tour.

Stage of drama,
in the velocity hum of the hum drum
the streets natural amphitheatre.
At dark,
alight to the heavens.

The day,
a Robin's cheerful free for all
the posh mans amused loud guffaw
an Arabic salutation call,
heard abound the city's living soul.

INTERVAL

On the uneven path, through the obstacles of trees with their own lines of records that are only an indicator of trials and troubles of the passage of time, the battleship- grey of the sky hints at the imminent conflict and war to come, before snow innocents the landscape and Spring forwards the thaw, when once more life sprouts and points bravely to witness the next fall and tumble of decades.

POLKA DOTTED PAPERS

It was threatening a storm of smoky,
heavy leaden purple,
then flash, clap and roll of cloudburst,

sheets of hail and obese water drops,
taking value from the retreating humid heat
added esteem to the afternoon storm.

Polaroid lightening, shocking, blinding,
your handful of poems now limply wet
and weeping from the onslaught.

They will revive, from beside the hearth.

ACKNOWLEDGEMENTS

A big thank you to Mark Davidson, at the most wonderful Hedgehog Press. To Pauline Sewards, Helen Sheppard and Stella Quinlivan of 'Satellite of Love' for their open, warm evenings and encouragement, who have given confidence to so many poets and story tellers. Also, other fantastic poetry events in Bristol like 'Spel', 'Berkeley Square Poetry Revue', 'Tonic', 'open collab' with Charlie and Jake and 'Lines of the Mind'. There are even more to suit every style of performance and atmosphere. Also my thanks to the Bristol Stanza Poetry Group who have helped me improve my poetry and I get to contribute suggestions and hear some fantastic poems of theirs in the bargain. Again to Pauline Seward who wrote my lovely blurb for the pamphlet. Lastly to Adam Crowther of BBC Radio Bristol Upload programme who has regularly broadcast my poetry and showcases the music and written talent in Bristol, it is a truly wonderful programme.

Cover Image is by Mrs Doris E Luxton (my Grandmother, Mary Caldwell's friend)

Thank you to the editors, who first published, placed and broadcast some of my poems in this pamphlet:

'Love is the Spirit of a Cat' first published in Acumen 101.
'We are who we are' first published in 'The Weather Indoors' by Tangent Books.
'Rose Bombs' first published in 'Dime Show Review' magazine and then 'Lyrically Justified, Volume 3' anthology by Arc.
'Beseeching' first published in Herheart poetry annual 2017.
'You Never Cry Alone' Broadcast on BBC Radio Bristol, Autumn 2020 and 'open collab' April 21 with Charlie and Jake who broadcast weaved improvised music and sonic landscapes.
'the answers' Highly Commended in the inaugural Bristol Cathedral Poetry Competition and published in their pamphlet.